<u>Dedication</u>

I would like to dedicate this book
to my Grandparents

Nana, Dadu, Amma and Nani
(Dr. Tapan, Ashitesh, Rina and Gargi)

You are as Bright as the Sun

This Book Belongs to

_____

Writer and Illustrator: Anushka Bhattacharjee

Cover Designer: Eduardo Paj

Editor: Cristy Watson

He created the BEAUTIFUL...

NEBULA

The Nebula was formed just like a...

Soon the Universe wanted a ball to play with.
The Nebula was turned into a **SUPER-HOT** ball!

Mr. Protostar was born...
Over time, I became the SUN you know today.
The GIGANTIC Ball of Gases.

I am at the **Center** of the **Solar System**
with **EIGHT Planets** revolving around me.

I NOURISH all LIFE on Earth.

Plants need my **SUNLIGHT** to make **FOOD** which starts the **FOOD CHAIN**.

Light from a bulb reaches your eyes in a
FRACTION of SECOND because it is close to you.

But the stars and I are far away,
so it takes longer for our light to reach you.

Scientists use **LIGHT YEARS** to measure **Distance** in **SPACE**.

1 Light Year = The distance light TRAVELS in ONE Year which is about **9,000,000,000,000** Kilometers.

I can eat more than **ONE MILLION** planets like Earth to fill my belly.

I AM ENORMOUS!

But I will not eat your EARTH.
I am a Friend and I give you **LIGHT** and **HEAT**.

But after those
precious minutes...

There would be **NO LIGHT.**
Earth would **FREEZE.**
All **LIFE** would **DISAPPEAR!**

The **PLANETS** would fly out of their **orbits**
And could **BUMP** into each other!

Earth would be set off on a straight course through space.
A **BLACK HOLE** could swallow the Earth...
Or a Friendly star might INVITE the Earth into its orbit!

But, you won't get to see what I look like when I am THAT OLD!
In a **Billion** years I will grow **HUGE** and I will shine even **BRIGHTER**!

After **FIVE Billion** years

I will turn into a

RED GIANT

and then

A WHITE DWARF.

About the Author

Anushka is 10 years old, and she is in grade five.

Anushka was born in Arkansas, then moved to Chicago, Dallas, and now lives in Toronto.

After writing fantasy stories, she wanted to write a STEM book that could help educate little kids.

She started reading at the age of two. She is an avid reader, has been a regular member of the local libraries since she was a toddler, and reads over 1000 library books in a year. While stuck at home during Covid-19, she wanted to do something constructive and that is how she nurtured the idea of writing books. She studies at Coronation School, where she has been selected for the "gifted program". Anushka enjoys bike riding and watching movies. She is also very good at ice skating. She has a sister, Arushi, who is in grade two.

Anushka has inspired many little readers during her in-person Book Events, who now want to pursue their dream of becoming an author. She has also inspired her sister, who started writing her own book at the age of five.

Anushka is very active in the community and donates part of her proceeds to charitable organizations like "Durham Children's Aid Association", "Hearth Place Cancer Support Centre", "Autism Home Base Durham Inc.", etc.

Connect with Anushka on Social Media

SOCIAL MEDIA LINK

1. Open your Phone Camera
2. Scan this QR
3. Click on the Link that pops up

https://www.instagram.com/ArushiAnushkaChildAuthors

https://www.facebook.com/ArushiAnushkaChildAuthors

CHILD AUTHORS

Published at Age 6 and 8

Story Books

Educational Books

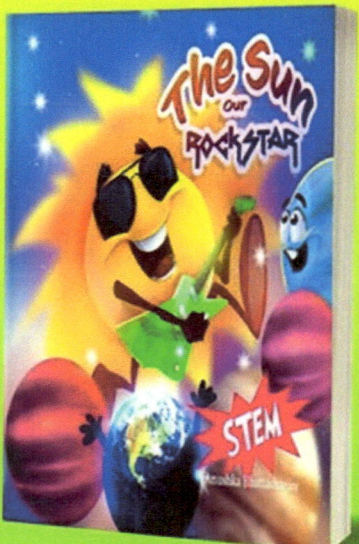

Activity Books

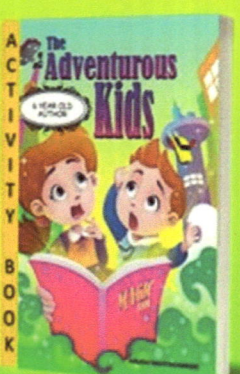

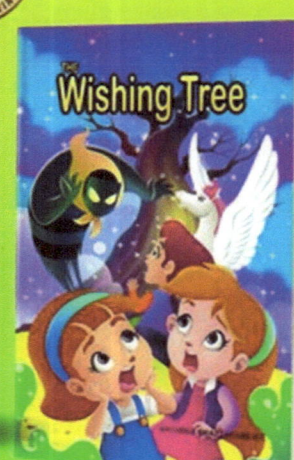

Indigo
amazon

BARNES & NOBLE

Special Thanks

To Anushka and Arushi's Art Teacher, Miss Eshita

Arushi - 6 year old

Anushka-10 year old